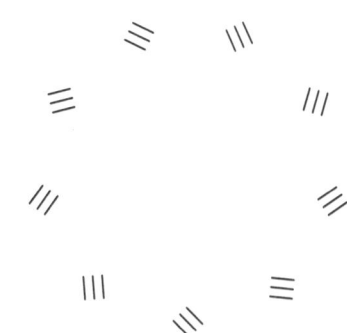

# The Community Practice

**A Four-Session Guide to Cultivating Community in the Way of Jesus**

WaterBrook

**John Mark Comer and Practicing the Way**

WaterBrook
An imprint of the Penguin Random House Christian Publishing Group,
a division of Penguin Random House LLC
1745 Broadway, New York, NY 10019
waterbrookmultnomah.com
penguinrandomhouse.com

A WaterBrook Trade Paperback Original

Published in association with Yates & Yates, www.yates2.com.

All photos courtesy of Practicing the Way.

Trade Paperback ISBN 978-0-593-60337-6
Ebook ISBN 978-0-593-60338-3

Printed in the United States of America on acid-free paper

1st Printing

Book and cover design by Practicing the Way.

For details on special quantity discounts for bulk purchases, contact specialmarketscms@penguinrandomhouse.com.

The authorized representative in the EU for product safety and compliance is Penguin Random House Ireland, Morrison Chambers, 32 Nassau Street, Dublin D02 YH68, Ireland. https://eu-contact.penguin.ie

# Contents

PART 01

# Getting Started

# Welcome

The modern world is facing a crisis of loneliness. The digital age has confused connectivity with community. Many of us ache to know and be known, to love and be loved, to belong to a family.

And yet we fear it, too, scared we'll get hurt, or be rejected, or feel constrained by commitment.

In our lonely age, Jesus' invitation is more provocative than ever before. His call to "come and follow" him is a call to join his community—which he likened to a family. Not a family in the modern Western imagination of mom, dad, and 2.5 kids, but in the ancient Mediterranean sense of a large, extended family of parents and grandparents and cousins and neighbors and co-workers and friends who aren't technically blood, yet are family—what sociologists call "fictive kinship groups" and the New Testament writers call "brothers and sisters."

But we won't find this kind of community just by attending church on Sunday. As important as it is to gather for worship with our local church, we each still have to find and form our own "fictive kinship group"—our own family within the larger village or tribe that is the church.

In this Practice, we will explore the key skills required to do this. It's not rocket science; it's as simple as sharing meals, building joyful connections, being vulnerable with one another about our sorrows and sins, and staying together when (not if) things get hard.

Living in community is not easy, and it won't just "happen" in our busy, disconnected world. It will require practice. But if you say *yes* to Jesus' invitation to become a part of his family, it has the potential to deeply change your life for the good.

Welcome to the Practice of community.

# The Nine Practices

SABBATH

PRAYER

FASTING

SOLITUDE

GENEROSITY

SCRIPTURE

COMMUNITY

SERVICE

WITNESS

Community is just one of nine core Practices in the body of resources available from Practicing the Way. The Practices are spiritual disciplines centered around the life rhythms of Jesus. They are designed not to add even more to your already overbusy life, but to slow you down and create space for the Spirit of God to form you to be with Jesus, become like him, and do what he did. Ultimately, they are a way to experience the love of God.

To run another Practice or learn more, turn to page 106.

# How to Use This Guide

## A few things you need to know

This Practice is designed to be done in community, whether with a few friends around a table, within your small group, in a larger class format, or with your entire church.

The Practice is four sessions long. We recommend meeting together every week or every other week. For those of you who want to spend more time on this Practice, we've included an additional four weeks of bonus conversations in the appendix to go deeper in Scripture and discussion. You are welcome to pause for these conversations in between sessions or skip over them.

You will all need a copy of this Companion Guide. You can purchase a print or ebook version from your preferred retailer or find a free digital PDF version at launch.practicingtheway.org. We recommend the print version so you can stay away from your devices during the Practices, as well as take notes during each session. But we realize that digital works better for some.

Each session should take about one to two hours, depending on how long you allow for discussion and whether or not you begin with a meal. See the sample session on the following page.

Are you a group leader or facilitator? Log in to your online Dashboard or sign up at launch.practicingtheway.org to find ideas, best practices, and tips on running this Practice. Page 110 also offers helpful information and tips on running this Practice.

Our Practices are designed to work in a variety of group sizes and environments. For that reason, your gatherings may include additional elements like meals or worship time or may follow a structure slightly different from the following sample. Please adapt as you see fit.

# Sample Session

Here is what a typical session could look like.

## Welcome
Welcome the group and open in prayer.

## Share a meal (60 min.)
Gather around a table to eat together and share a conversation.

## Introduction (2–3 min.)
Watch the introduction to the session and pause the video when indicated for your first discussion.

## Discussion 01: Practice reflection in triads (15–20 min.)
Process your previous week's spiritual exercise in smaller groups of three to five people with the questions in the Guide.

## Teaching (20 min.)
Watch the teaching portion of the video.

## Discussion 02: Group conversation (15–30 min.)
Pause the video when indicated for a group-wide conversation.

## Testimony and tutorial (5–10 min.)
Watch the rest of the video.

## Prayer to close
Close by praying the liturgy in the Guide, or however you choose.

# The Weekly Rhythm

The four sessions of this Practice are designed to follow a four-part rhythm that is based on our model of spiritual formation.

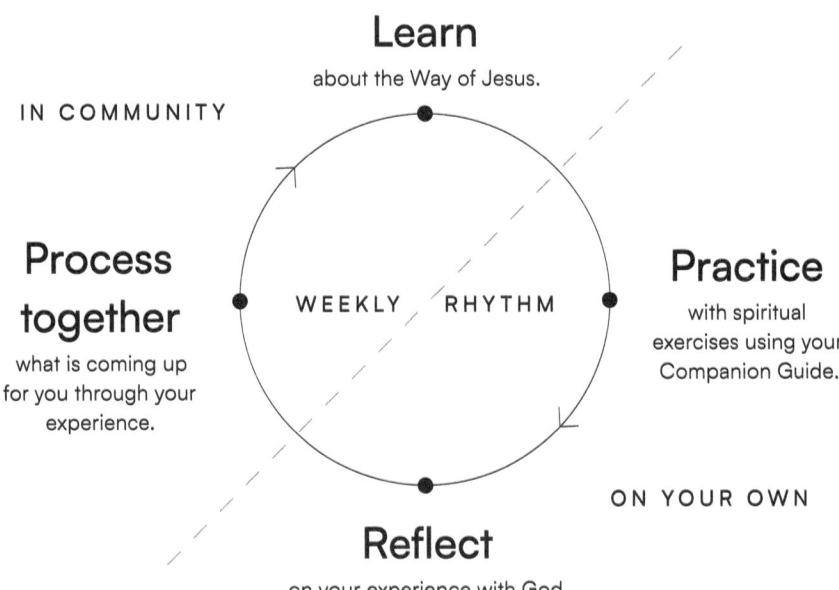

**Learn**
about the Way of Jesus.

IN COMMUNITY

**Process together**
what is coming up for you through your experience.

WEEKLY RHYTHM

**Practice**
with spiritual exercises using your Companion Guide.

ON YOUR OWN

**Reflect**
on your experience with God.

## 01  Learn

Gather together as a community for an interactive experience of learning about the Way of Jesus through teaching, storytelling, and discussion. Bring your Guide to the session and follow along.

## 02  Practice

On your own, before the next session, go and "put it into practice,"* as Jesus himself said. We will provide weekly spiritual exercises to integrate this practice into your everyday life, as well as recommended resources to go deeper.

## 03  Reflect

Reflection is key to spiritual formation. After your practice and before the next session, set aside 10–15 minutes to reflect on your experience. Reflection questions are included in this Guide at the end of each session.

## 04  Process together

When you come back together, watch the introduction, and then start by sharing your reflections with your group. This moment is crucial because we need one another to process our lives before God and make sense of our stories. If you are meeting in a larger group, you will need to break into smaller subgroups for this conversation so everyone has a chance to share.

---

* Philippians 4v9.

# Tips on Beginning a New Practice

This Guide is full of spiritual exercises, time-tested strategies, and good advice on the spiritual discipline of community.

But it's important to note that the Practices are not formulaic. We can't use them to control our spiritual formation, or even our relationship with God. Sometimes they don't even work very well. Over the coming weeks, there may be some days when you feel more deeply known and loved in your relationships than you ever have, and others where it just feels frustrating, ordinary, or even painful. That's normal.

The key with all the spiritual disciplines is to let go of outcomes and just offer them up to Jesus in love.

Because it's so easy to lose sight of the ultimate aim of a Practice, here are a few tips to keep in mind as you begin living more deeply in community.

## 01  Start small

Start where you are, not where you "should" be. It's counterintuitive, but the smaller the start, the better chance you have of really sticking to it and growing over time. It's better to integrate relationships into your life slowly than to commit to an ambitious social schedule that asks too much of you too soon and risks burning you out a few weeks in.

## 02  Think subtraction, not addition

The goal here isn't to add social events and obligations to your already overbusy, overfull life. You are likely already overwhelmed. Instead, think: *How am I currently living independently or even in isolation, and is there an opportunity there to live more relationally instead?* Formation is about less, not more. About slowing down and simplifying your life around what matters most: life with Jesus, done in community.

## 03  You get out what you put in

The more fully you give yourself to this Practice, the more life-changing it will be; the more you just dabble in it, the more shortcuts you take, the less of an effect it will have on your transformation. It's up to you: We make invitations; you make decisions.

## 04  Remember the J curve

Experts on learning tell us that whenever we set out to master a new skill, it tends to follow a J-shaped curve; we tend to get worse before we get better. If you are introverted, socially anxious, or have been hurt by your community before, this may be especially true. This Practice might feel a bit difficult at first; it will get easier over time. Spiritual formation, the process of becoming people of love, requires community. So just stay with the Practice.

## 05  There is no formation without repetition

Spiritual formation is slow, deep, cumulative work that happens over years, not weeks. The goal of this four-week experience is just to get you started on a journey of a lifetime. Upon completion of this Practice, you will have a map for the journey ahead, and hopefully some possible companions for the Way.

But what you do next is up to you.

# Before You Begin

The following resources are designed to enhance your experience of the Community Practice, but they are entirely optional.

## Recommended reading

Reading a book alongside the Community Practice can greatly enhance your understanding and enjoyment of this discipline. You may love to read, or you may not. For that reason, it's recommended, but certainly not required.

The recommended reading for the Community Practice is *Made to Belong* by David Kim.

David Kim is a pastor, author, and speaker passionate about Jesus and all things discipleship, formation, and community.

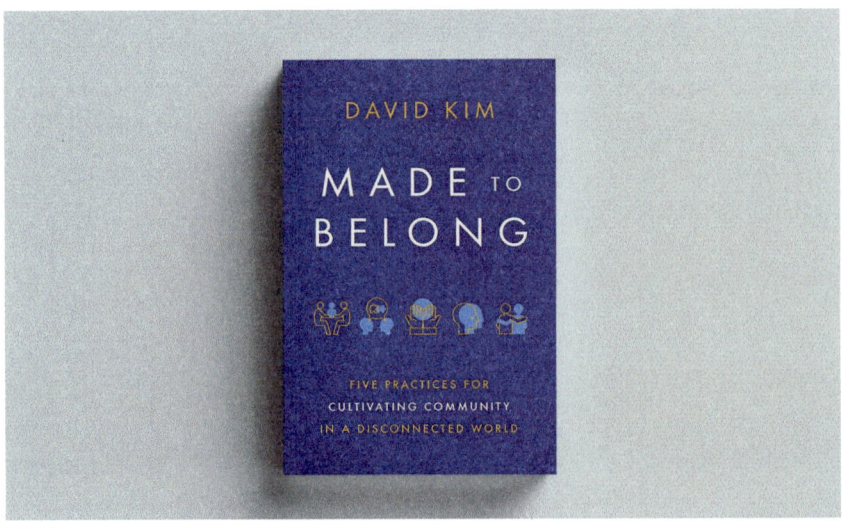

# Table Conversations

Table Conversations includes 100 curated questions divided into two sets: "Start Small" contains simpler prompts for groups getting to know each other, while "Go Deeper" contains more probing questions around life, faith, and formation.

Learn more at practicingtheway.org/tableconversations.

# The Spiritual Health Reflection

One final note: Before you begin Session 01, please set aside 20–30 minutes and take the Spiritual Health Reflection. This is a self-assessment we developed in partnership with pastors and leading experts in spiritual formation. It's designed to help you reflect on the health of your soul in order to better name Jesus' invitations to you as you follow the Way.

You can come back to the Spiritual Health Reflection as often as you'd like (we recommend one to two times a year) to chart your growth and continue to move forward on your spiritual journey.

To access the Spiritual Health Reflection, visit practicingtheway.org/reflection and create an account. Answer the prompt questions slowly and prayerfully.

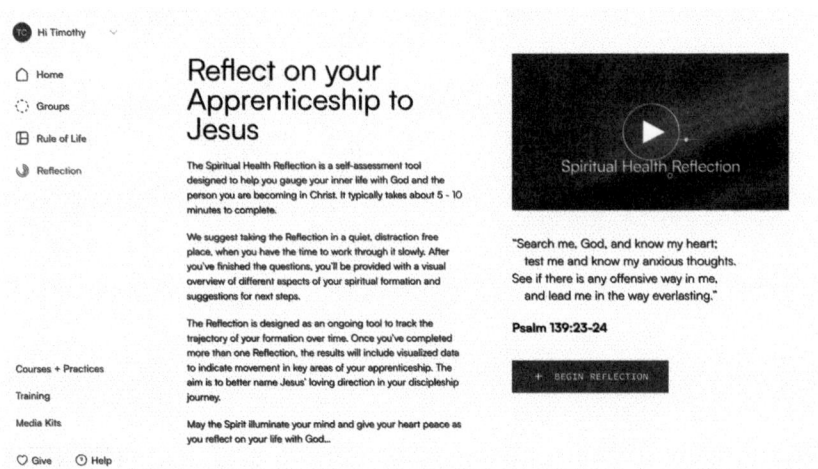

# The Practicing the Way Primer

If this is your first time engaging with a Practicing the Way resource, we invite you to set aside 15 minutes before Session 01 to watch a primer on spiritual formation. This will give you a brief overview of the "why" behind spiritual practices and key insights to guard and guide your coming practice.

Log in to your online Dashboard, or sign up to watch the primer at launch.practicingtheway.org.

PART 02

# The Sessions

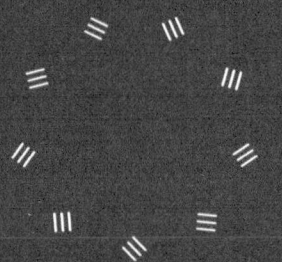

# Be Family
# Around a Table

# Overview

Throughout the library of Scripture, there is a recurring theme of a feast. Picture a table filled with food and drink, where the family of God—every tribe, tongue, and nation—is gathered together singing, laughing, and giving thanks to God the Father. One diverse but unified family under God.

Yet today most if not all of us in the West would say we experience being formed away from a table and community like this, rather than being drawn toward it. Radical individualism is the dominant experience of our day, and it's breeding a widespread feeling that, though we are more connected than we have ever been, we are also lonelier than ever.

In our culture, living in regular, intentional community is a vital act of counter-formation and a radical witness to our surrounding culture. But this invitation to community is about more than weekly attendance at a Sunday service—as important as that is. It's an invitation to live deeply into a new family based not on blood, background, or biases, but on our shared apprenticeship to Jesus.

And the life of this new family starts at one ordinary, level place: the table.

# Opening Questions

When instructed, circle up in triads (smaller groups of three to five people) and discuss the following questions:

01   What brought you to the Community Practice? What are you hoping to see God do in your life through it?

02   What is one question you would like to explore in this Practice?

03   What's your primary feeling around living more deeply in community? Excitement? Hesitance? Fear?

04   Share about a time when you felt a strong sense of belonging in a particular group or community. What made that experience memorable for you?

# Teaching

## Key Scripture

Genesis 1v26–27

## Session summary

- Spiritual formation—the process of becoming people of love—occurs primarily within community.

- Community is emphasized all throughout Scripture:

  - We are created in the image of a Trinitarian God.

  - Jesus called disciples (plural), not just one (singular), to join his new community, the church.

  - The church is to be like a family based not on blood, but on apprenticeship to him.

  - This family is to be like an ancient Mediterranean kinship group.

- We can categorize this new family into four circles of community:

01 **Our brothers and sisters (or intimates):** One to five close relationships who deeply know us and love us as we are

02 **Our kin:** About 15 family members and friends who are like family, sharing life and supporting one another

03 **Our village:** Up to 150 broader connections providing a social network for support and resources

04 **Our tribe:** The larger group we identify with, such as our church, where we find purpose and community

- While we need all four circles, our deepest formation, healing, and growth occur in the inner circles.

- The best way to start building these inner circles is to start gathering a small group of people around a table for a regular meal.

# Teaching Notes

# Discussion Questions

Now it's time for a conversation about the teaching. Pause the video for a few minutes to discuss in small groups:

01 What examples of radical individualism have you seen at play around you, or even in your own life?

02 What are the most common barriers you personally face to living more deeply in community?

03 What most stood out to you about the four circles of community?

04 For week one, the exercise is to share a meal together. What were meals around the table like with your family, and how might that influence your view of this exercise?

# Practice Notes

As you continue to watch Session 01 together, feel free to use this page to take notes.

# Closing Prayer

Take a few deep breaths, become aware of God's presence, and pray this prayer slowly, leaving a short silence between each line.

Jesus Christ, you have called us
your brothers and sisters, giving us
a home and a place of belonging.
Help us to say *yes* to it, and to
make room for one another at
the table of your love—in our homes,
in our schedules, and in our hearts.

Amen.

# Exercise

## Share a meal together.

We invite you to begin each session by sharing a meal together as the baseline for the remainder of the Practice. You may already share a weekly meal with another group, such as a home community or small group. In that case, feel free to adapt this Practice to your own life. But if at all possible, begin each of the next three sessions by sharing a meal together.

As you plan for your weekly meal, keep these tips in mind:

01 **Choose your places:** Decide on the location or locations where you will host your dinners.

02 **Set a consistent day and time:** Choose a specific day and time each week that works for everyone, ideally before each of the remaining sessions.

03 **Organize a potluck-style meal:** Have everyone sign up for specific elements (mains, desserts, drinks). Be mindful of any dietary restrictions in the group.

04 **Encourage contributions beyond food:** Participants can also help with setting and cleaning up.

# Community

O Triune God,
Father,
Son,
Holy Spirit—the joyful relationship
at the center of the universe.

Let us not be mistaken to think
that the ordinary nature of this gathering
means you are not here.

Meet us, O Lord, in every curious question,
honest prayer, and offering of attention.

May we share in your life
as we now share in one another's.

For some, the table brings memories of
connection and plenty;
for others, absence and lack.

Grant us compassion, O Lord.

May the table we set be wide enough
for all these stories.

Open our hearts to love today, knowing
that in receiving our brother, our sister,
we are surely receiving you.

Amen.

# Reach Exercise

We recognize that we're all at different stages of discipleship and seasons of life. To that end, we've added a Reach Exercise to each of the four sessions for those who have the time, energy, and desire to go further in the Community Practice.

This week, we have a guided reflection designed to help you identify whom God may be drawing you to be family with. Some people call this "spiritual adoption," which is a way of talking about how the Spirit of God will often gently move our hearts toward particular people to be family with.

You should come out of this exercise with a clearer sense of who your "kin" could be and what the right next steps are for you.

## Part 01: The four domains of life

Consider the four domains of life on the following page.

01   Begin by inviting the Holy Spirit to fill your mind and guide your imagination through this exercise.

02   Go through each domain and write down the names of anyone you know. You don't need to make an exhaustive list; simply write down any relationships that come to mind, from a lifelong best friend to a casual acquaintance.

03   Now go back through each list slowly and circle any names you feel your heart drawn to. You're not committing to anything right now, just exercising holy imagination. Listen to the Spirit in your heart, gently instructing the desires of your heart.

| Church | Work |
|---|---|
| **Third spaces**<br>(your gym, school, book club, coffee shop, etc.) | **Family and friends** |

# Part 02: The four circles of community

In this session, we covered the research of Dr. Robert Dunbar on the four circles of relationship, based on differing group size and levels of vulnerability. This exercise is an attempt to map your current relationships on this grid.

01    Pause again and invite the Holy Spirit to fill your mind and guide your thinking.

02    Go through each circle and write down the names of anyone you are already in relationship with in that sphere.

03    Pause to evaluate these questions:

- Are there any areas where you are missing relationships? For example, you may have lots of family and friends but few intimates, or you may have two or three close brothers or sisters but be lacking a larger village to draw on in times of need. Where do you need to add to your community?

- Are there any areas where you are overextended? Where do you have too many relational commitments? For example, you may be trying to go deeper with seven different people, when you really have the capacity for only two or three. Where do you need to subtract from your community? (To clarify, we're not talking about rejecting or hurting people, but about graciously pulling back from relationships that are beyond your limitations.)

04    Now go back through your four-domains worksheet. Move any names you circled over to this four-circles worksheet. Place a question mark after each name you transfer. You're not committing to anything right now, just dreaming with God about a possible future.

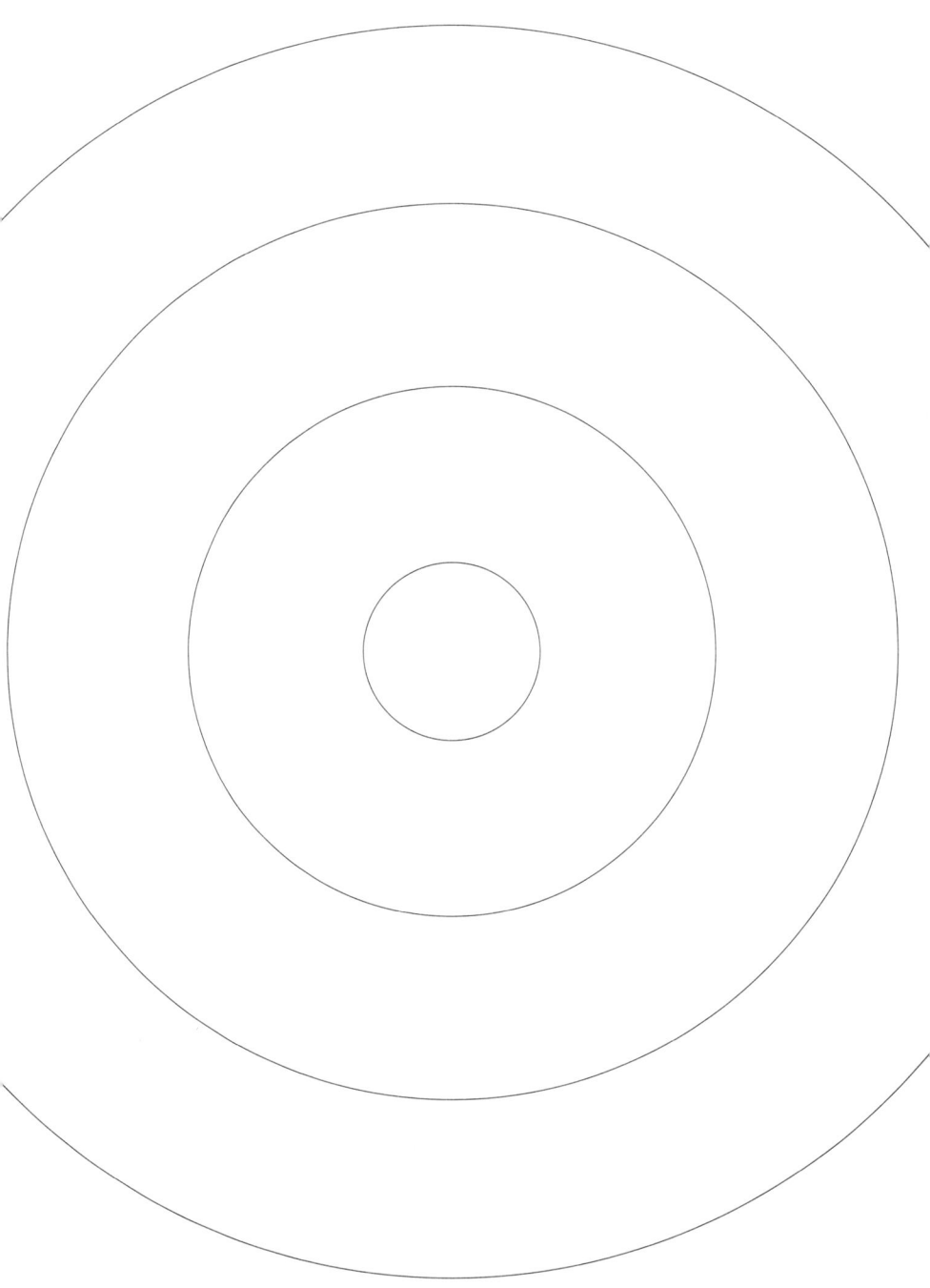

**Be Family Around a Table**

Pause to prayerfully listen for God's direction:

01  God, who of these precious people are you
    highlighting right now?

02  God, what next steps do you want me to take with
    each person?

03  God, what areas of my relational life need change,
    healing, or attention?

# Part 03: Finding and forming your own kinship group

Now let's zoom in on circle two—your kin, or family, in the Way of Jesus.

**If you are a part of a healthy biological family following Jesus together, reflect on these questions** (if not, move to the next section):

01    In the smaller box, write down the names of your biological family members that you are intentionally following Jesus with. This may look like being in a home community together, attending the same church, or doing regular family meals together. Include your spouse, children, parents, siblings, etc.

02    To the side, write down what gifts, strengths, and resources your family has to offer others—this could be a home to meet in, money to buy food, ability to cook meals, a spare room, hard-won wisdom, a stable marriage, etc. No family is perfect, but what is your family's offering?

03    In the larger box, write down the names of people God may be spiritually adopting into your family to become "kin." Think of friends who could become like your brothers and sisters if you were to go deeper together. Think of people in other stages of life (young single people if you're middle aged and married, or older couples if you're younger). Especially think of any friend who doesn't have a family like yours, either because of geography (their family is far away), spirituality (their family doesn't follow Jesus), tragedy (they've lost their family, are a widow or widower, or are fatherless, motherless, or an orphan), or any reason at all. Whom may God be drawing you into a closer relationship with?

04   To the side, write down their gifts, strengths, and resources they could contribute to your family. For example, if you have kids, they may love being around twenty-somethings from your church who become like aunties or uncles or older siblings.

**If you are single or married but not a part of a healthy biological family following Jesus together, reflect on these questions:**

01   In the smaller box, write down the name of a biological family you find yourself drawn to. This could be a family you know through your church, or home community, that you feel an affinity of heart toward.

02   In the larger box, write down your group of friends that you may loosely follow Jesus with, especially if they, too, are drawn to the same biological family.

03   Below the boxes, write down what steps you could take to move toward the family you named. This could look like offering to babysit for a date night, inviting yourself over for dinner, taking their family on a picnic, or asking one of the parents to get coffee with you for mentorship.

04   Then, write down what steps your friend group could take to begin to operate more like a family. This could look like eating a weekly meal, moving in together, going on vacation together, adopting a biological family into your group, etc.

To end this Reach Exercise, spend a little time in prayerful reflection. You don't need to do anything just yet. Sit with these worksheets over the coming four weeks of this Practice. Continue to write down names or make notes as thoughts come to mind you feel are from the Spirit. Pay close attention to the movements of your heart. Keep your eyes open. Continue to listen for where God is leading you.

Family

Kin

Next steps

# Practice Reflection

Reflection is a key component in our spiritual formation.

Millennia ago, King David prayed in Psalm 139v23–24:

> Search me, God, and know my heart;
>     test me and know my anxious thoughts.
> See if there is any offensive way in me,
>     and lead me in the way everlasting.

South African professor Trevor Hudson has quoted one of his pastoral supervisors as saying, "We do not learn from experience; we learn from reflection upon experience."*

If you want to get the most out of this Practice, you need to do it and then reflect on it.

————————————

\* Trevor Hudson, *A Mile in My Shoes: Cultivating Compassion* (Upper Room Books, 2005), 57.

> Before your next time together with the group for Session 02, take 10–15 minutes to journal your answers to the following three questions:

## 01  Where did I feel resistance?

## 02  Where did I feel joy?

## 03  Where did I most experience God's nearness?

*Note: As you write, be as specific as possible. While bullet points are just fine, if you write your insights out in narrative form, your brain will be able to process them in a more lasting way.*

# Reflection Notes

# Keep Growing (Optional)

The following resources were created to enhance your experience of this Practice, but they are entirely optional.

##  Read

*Made to Belong* by David Kim (Chapters 01–02)

## ılılı Listen

*Rule of Life* podcast on community (Episode 01)

## ▤ Bonus Conversation

If you would like to slow down this four-week Practice to give your community more time to sit in each week's teaching and spiritual exercise, you can pause and meet for an optional conversation as outlined in the appendix.

# Share Your Joys
# and Sorrows

# Overview

The Lord's Supper began as a full meal, centered around Jesus, done together in community in joyful celebration of his life, death, and resurrection. At the heart of the table was a deep and honest communion with God and with one another.

We all know the experience of sitting at a table with other well-meaning disciples of Jesus and feeling the opposite of communion—uncertainty about how to bring the deeper, more honest parts of our lives to the table, as conversation more naturally stays at the surface. But we were made to share our lives—our delights and burdens—with others and to experience the joy and comfort of being known.

Our tables can become places for more than good food and interesting anecdotes; they can be settings where we honestly bring our joys and sorrows to those whom we love and who love us—a place of genuine communion.

# Reflection Questions

When instructed, circle up in triads (smaller groups of three to five people) and discuss the following questions:

01  What did your experience of sharing a meal together this week look like, and how was it for you?

02  How does the prospect of sharing a weekly meal make you feel? Intimidated? Excited? Anxious?

03  How social do you consider yourself to be, and how does that influence your desire or capacity for sharing a weekly meal in community?

04  What is one thing you can do to improve your preparation and planning for the next meal you share?

# Teaching

## Key Scripture

Mark 14v22–24

## Session summary

- The ultimate goal of sharing a meal together is for the table to become a place of communion with God and with one another.

- We experience this communion when we share our joys and sorrows with a community that is growing in love and trust.

- We share our joys because:

  - God is the most joyful being in all the universe, and he designed our lives together to be built around joy.

  - Joy is not our default state, and so, to become people of joy, we require "the discipline of celebration."

  - Joy is an act of defiance in a culture of fear and outrage.

- We share our sorrows because:

  - We are not built to carry our wounds, fears, and needs on our own.

  - Even Jesus modeled the importance of inviting friends into our sorrows in the Garden of Gethsemane.

  - The single most important factor in determining whether our pain shatters or strengthens us is whether or not it finds "a relational home" in community.

- While this takes trust and time, the best place to start is by doing life together around a table and beginning to share honestly as you do.

# Teaching Notes

As you watch Session 02 together, feel free to use these pages to take notes.

# Discussion Questions

Now it's time for a conversation about the teaching. Pause the video for a few minutes to discuss in small groups:

01   As you listened, what most stood out to you?

02   Does the act of celebrating—whether it is celebrating yourself or someone else—feel natural or unnatural to you? Why?

03   On a scale of 1 to 10, where 10 represents complete transparency and 1 represents no transparency, how transparent are you in your current relationships? Why do you think that is?

04   Reflect on a positive and a negative experience you have had sharing your burdens in a relationship or group. What made the difference?

# Practice Notes

As you continue to watch Session 02 together, feel free to use this page to take notes.

_____

_____

_____

_____

_____

_____

_____

_____

_____

_____

_____

_____

_____

_____

_____

_____

_____

_____

_____

_____

_____

_____

_____

_____

_____

_____

_____

# Closing Prayer

Take a few deep breaths, become aware of God's presence, and pray this prayer slowly, leaving a short silence between each line.

God, you held nothing of yourself
back from us, sharing your life,
your heart, your feasts, and your
sorrows. Help us to do the same with
one another now, braving vulnerability,
and experiencing the liberation of
finding true belonging, today.

Amen.

# Exercise

## At your next weekly meal, go around the table and share the highs and lows of the week.

- Your highs could be what you're grateful for, excited about, or currently finding joy in.

- Your lows could be what you're grieving, what you're fearful about, or a moment that was difficult for you during the week.

- Regardless of what your high or low is, be honest and let your community into what you're celebrating and what you're finding challenging.

# Reach Exercise

Get together with a trusted friend and share honestly about a struggle you're currently facing—whether that's a wound, a fear, or a need.

- This might be a struggle that you don't yet feel comfortable sharing with a larger group during your weekly meal.

- Rather than holding it inside, set up a coffee or tea date with a trusted friend and bare your heart to them.

- Or turn it around and, if you want to offer support to someone else, consider reaching out to a friend who is in a difficult season and encouraging them.

# Practice Reflection

Before your next time together with the group for Session 03, take 10–15 minutes to journal your answers to the following three questions:

01  What did I find most difficult about this exercise?

02  What emotions did I experience in sharing my joys and sorrows?

03  How do I sense the Spirit inviting me deeper into honesty in community going forward?

*Note: As you write, be as specific as possible. While bullet points are just fine, if you write your insights out in narrative form, your brain will be able to process them in a more lasting way.*

# Reflection Notes

# Keep Growing (Optional)

The following resources were created to enhance your experience of this
Practice, but they are entirely optional.

## 📖 Read

*Made to Belong* by David Kim (Chapters 03–05)

## 𝅘𝅥𝅮 Listen

*Rule of Life* podcast on community (Episode 02)

## 🗨 Bonus Conversation

If you would like to slow down this four-week Practice to give your
community more time to sit in each week's teaching and spiritual exercise,
you can pause and meet for an optional conversation as outlined in the
appendix.

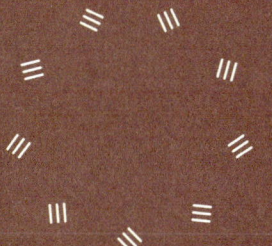

# Confess Your Sins

# Overview

There is an age-old enemy to life in community that holds more power than the modern deterrents of digital distraction and transience. Its roots can be traced all the way back, before cellphones and cities, to the garden days in *The Book of Genesis*.

It's the ancient enemy of shame.

Shame is the great disconnector between us and God, and us and one another; it fosters and follows the life of sin. It's what makes all of us wonder, *Would I be loved if they really knew me?* While Jesus and his Gospel have answered this question with an emphatic *yes*, we still have a part to play in order to truly hear that word in our shadows; that part, in the language of Scripture, is to "confess our sins."*

While the practice of confession is not a silver bullet, it is one of the most powerful tools we have to deal a lethal blow to this ancient enemy of shame and open ourselves up to experience what our hearts most long for—the healing love of God and community.

---

* 1 John 1v9.

# Reflection Questions

When instructed, circle up in triads (smaller groups of three to five people) and discuss the following questions:

01  How did it go sharing your highs and lows around the table at your last meal?

02  Where did you personally experience resistance while sharing your own highs and lows?

03  How did this exercise shift the dynamic or sense of connection in the group for the remainder of your time together?

04  This week's skill for living in community is confessing your sins. How would you describe your experience with confession?

# Teaching

## Key Scripture

Romans 7v21–25, 8v1–2

## Session summary

- While there are many challenges to living in community—busyness, transience, distraction, flakiness, emotional immaturity—there is no challenge greater than that of shame.

- Shame is a:

  - fear that you are unlovable as you really are.

  - disconnector from yourself, others, and God.

  - by-product of sin, and often a cause of sin.

- We deal with shame through the practice of confession.

- Confession is naming the sin done by you, to you, and around you to a loving community or "confessor."

- A confessor is anyone who you trust to proclaim God's love and truth to you in your sin.

- If shame is a disconnector between us and God, and us and one another, confession is the great reconnector.

# Teaching Notes

As you watch Session 03 together, feel free to use these pages to take notes.

# Discussion Questions

Now it's time for a conversation about the teaching. Pause the video for a few minutes to discuss in small groups:

01  Where did you feel challenged or invited as you listened?

02  What do you notice about how shame affects your interactions with God and others?

03  What thoughts or feelings emerge when you consider the possibility of being "fully known and fully loved" in community?

04  In what ways do you think the Gospel influences how we confess or receive someone else's confession?

# Practice Notes

As you continue to watch Session 03 together, feel free to use this page to take notes.

# Closing Prayer

**End your time together by praying this liturgy:**

Help us, Father, to not live in the
shadows of shame and fear, nor
to believe in the lie we're unwanted
or unlovable. Teach us to share the
load, and to help others release theirs,
so that in confessing and receiving one
another, we may be more like you in
this world.

Amen.

# Exercise

## Find a confessor and confess your sins.

You may not call this person "a confessor." Maybe they're a trusted friend, pastor, mentor, therapist, or spiritual director—anyone whom you feel safe with and believe would love you no matter what.

- Ask them to get together and let them know you want to share how you're really doing.

- You can start small by just naming an ongoing struggle in your life. Or, depending on the level of trust and the relationship, you can lay it all bare and tell them something you've been hiding for years, like an addiction, abortion, or affair.

- Be discerning in what you share, but we invite you to be courageous in taking this step deeper into community and toward healing.

And if you're the one receiving the confession:

- Listen with attention, attunement, and a heart of compassion. When they are done, you can say, "In Christ's name, you are forgiven."

- If you want, you can also say something like, "I've never loved you as much as I love you right now." Community is the place where we come out of hiding and experience the love of God through one another.

# Reach Exercise

## Explore forming what John Wesley and the Methodists called a discipleship band.

This is a triad of around three people (five people is the absolute max) who meet regularly for prayer and confession.

Your band could consist of a subgroup of your weekly table community or small group, or totally different people. While it's ideal to be together in person, your band can also meet digitally, which makes it possible to join with close friends who may live farther away.

Just like a weekly meal is the optimal way to build the kinship layer of community into your Rule of Life or your regular routine, a discipleship band is a way to build that more intimate layer of brothers and sisters into your Rule of Life as well.

Our friends from the modern Methodist church have put together a great primer on how to start and run your own discipleship band that you can download for free. They've also created an app you can use to keep your group on track.

To form your own band:

01   Go to discipleshipbands.com, download the free ebook, and give it a read.

02   Identify and invite a few others to start a band with you. (It may be ideal if your band is a subgroup of your kinship group or home community, simply because it's fewer relationships to stay up to date with.)

03   Put a date on the calendar and begin meeting regularly to talk through the simple questions in the ebook, which can also be found on the following page.

- How is it with your soul?

- What are your struggles and successes?

- How might the Word and Spirit be speaking in your life?

- Do you have any sin that you want to confess?

- Are there any secrets or hidden things you would like to share?

# Practice Reflection

Before your next time together with the group for Session 04, take 10–15 minutes to journal your answers to the following three questions:

01   Where did I feel resistance in confession?

02   Which emotions did I expect to experience? Which were I surprised by?

03   In what ways did I encounter God as I confessed my sins?

*Note: As you write, be as specific as possible. While bullet points are just fine, if you write your insights out in narrative form, your brain will be able to process them in a more lasting way.*

# Reflection Notes

# Keep Growing (Optional)

The following resources were created to enhance your experience of this Practice, but they are entirely optional.

📖 **Read**

*Made to Belong* by David Kim (Chapters 06–07)

ıllıll **Listen**

*Rule of Life* podcast on community (Episode 03)

💬 **Bonus Conversation**

If you would like to slow down this four-week Practice to give your community more time to sit in each week's teaching and spiritual exercise, you can pause and meet for an optional conversation as outlined in the appendix.

# Stay Together
# to Grow

# Overview

In the first century, no one had witnessed a community like the church of Jesus. They weren't related by blood, ethnicity, or class, and yet they were a family. At their tables, men and women were treated equally. They shared everything. They bore witness to the power of the resurrected Jesus.

But they were also a mess.

We need only read the New Testament letters to see that these communities were riddled with imperfections. They were real people with real problems.

In the same way that we tend to draw an overidealized picture of the Early Church, we can have a romanticized vision for our own community—one that unfortunately leaves many of us disillusioned and disappointed. As we aim to mature in our discipleship to Jesus, we must all come to terms with this: There is no avoiding real people with real problems. In fact, that is the only context where we will truly be formed into people of love.

What we need is a better vision: a vision to stay in community.

# Reflection Questions

When instructed, circle up in triads (smaller groups of three to five people) and discuss the following questions:

01  Share your experience confessing your sins this week.

02  What would need to happen for you to make confession a more regular rhythm in your life?

03  How did the act of confession impact your sense of shame or disconnection from God?

04  What has this experience shown you about how to confess and how to receive someone else's confession well?

# Teaching

## Key Scripture

1 Corinthians 3v1–4

## Session summary

- Though the Early Church was a revolutionary and compelling example of community, they were also real people with real problems.

- Our idealized visions of community often prevent us from staying to foster real community.

- Living in Christian community is difficult because:

  - It is not centered on shared opinions or preferences but on our shared apprenticeship to Jesus.

  - Living in close proximity to others leaves us vulnerable to wound and be wounded.

- We grow into people of love in community when we accept its imperfect nature.

- If we determine it's time to leave a community, we must end well and in a way that allows us to reengage with another community healthily.

- There are two primary reasons to stay in community:

  - It takes a long time to build a deep community.

  - We need this kind of deep, long-term community to grow.

- In order to stay in community, we must:

  - Deal with conflict.

  - Practice forgiveness.

  - Commit to never stop growing.

- The goal is for God's thoughts to become deeply imprinted in our minds so that, in both challenging times and moments of joy, we begin to think and feel as he does, seeing the world through his eyes and responding as he would if he were us.

# Teaching Notes

As you watch Session 04 together, feel free to use these pages to take notes.

# Discussion Questions

Now it's time for a conversation about the teaching. Pause the video for a few minutes to discuss in small groups:

01  As you listened, what resonated with your heart and mind?

02  How have you experienced the consequences of idealizing community, either personally or from someone else?

03  What stood out to you about the six-stage Cycle of Community?

04  What are the primary challenges or temptations you face related to staying in community?

# Practice Notes

As you continue to watch Session 04 together, feel free to use this page to take notes.

# Closing Prayer

**End your time together by praying this liturgy:**

Help us, Father, to be real with
one another, to be real about
what it means to be one body,
and to stay in persevering love
with one another as we pursue
your presence, your kingdom,
your love.

Amen.

# Exercise

Now it's time to translate the last four weeks of learning and practice into a plan. What are the right next steps for living in community? What is the Spirit stirring in your heart? Whom is God "spiritually adopting" you to?

The following reflection questions are designed to help you discern God's invitations to you in the next stage of your spiritual journey.

- Pause for a moment to quiet yourself before God. Take a few deep breaths. Let yourself come to stillness.

- Invite the Holy Spirit to fill your mind and imagination, and guide your heart into his will.

- Then, prayerfully reflect on the following questions:

## 01  Start by closing your eyes and imagining your life three to five years from now.

## 02  What's your ideal vision of living in community?

How do you dream of doing life in a more relational way? What kind of close friends do you have? What does your kinship group look like? What kind of rhythms do you live by? How do you move through life together? Just dream for a few moments and write down your preferred future.

## 03 What next steps do you sense the Spirit inviting you to take to move toward this vision?

These could be something like getting coffee with an acquaintance to see if they could become a closer friend; inviting a family over for dinner; talking to your friends about forming a kinship group or table community; meeting with a confessor, etc. They are likely small. Write down two to three next steps.

## 04 Revisit the Four Circles of Community chart on page 35.

Prayerfully consider the names with question marks. Through this Practice, has the Spirit continued to place any of these names on your heart? Is there anyone you can remove the question mark from?

## 05 For those with question marks still remaining, is there any next step you sense the Spirit inviting you to take with them specifically?

(Getting coffee, sharing a meal, having a hard conversation, etc.)

## 06  Now think about each circle and your Rule of Life, or your regular routines.

Do you have an intentional meeting with each group in your schedule? If so, write it down. (For example, you could write down church on Sunday under village or tribe, Tuesday night dinner under kinship group/community, and Saturday morning discipleship band under intimates.) If not, do you feel any leading to begin meeting with a group more intentionally? Write down a possible plan.

## 07  Now revisit the Kinship chart on page 39.

Prayerfully review. Are there any names you want to add or subtract?

## 08  What are the invitations of the Spirit to you?

What next steps do you sense a leading to take to turn the idea of a kinship group into a reality?

End by quietly offering your dreams, desires, questions, and fears to God. Ask him, who **"sets the solitary in families,"**\* to pastor you into community and incrementally shape you into a person of love.

---

\* Psalm 68v6 (NKJV).

# Keep Growing (Optional)

The following resources were created to enhance your experience of this Practice, but they are entirely optional.

## 📖 Read

*Made to Belong* by David Kim (Chapters 08–10 and Conclusion)

## ᵢₗₗᵢ Listen

*Rule of Life* podcast on community (Episode 04)

## 💬 Bonus Conversation

If you would like to slow down this four-week Practice to give your community more time to sit in each week's teaching and spiritual exercise, you can pause and meet for an optional conversation as outlined in the appendix.

May God who "sets the solitary in families" make you into a family.

May he bind your hearts together in his love.

May he heal you, grow you, and form you into people of love.

PART 03

# Continue the Journey

# Further Practice

You are not going to find and form a kinship group in four weeks. This short Practice is designed only to get you moving on a lifelong journey. The weekly rhythm of sharing a meal that you've been practicing is meant to be integrated into your Rule of Life, should you so choose. You may choose to make a weekly community meal a rhythmic part of your discipleship, or you may want to find another pathway into community.

Where you go from here is entirely up to you, but here are a few ideas of how you could go deeper into community.

01 **Go on a retreat with your group:** Find a cabin in the woods, book an Airbnb in the sun, or reserve space at a local retreat center, and go away for a few days with your community. Find something meaningful to fill your time—hearing from an older, wiser mentor in the faith, hosting deep conversations, prophetically praying over one another, etc. Make sure you eat lots of meals and find time to play together to joyfully connect.

02 **Go on vacation together:** Go camping or take a road trip or do whatever you love to do to rest, but try doing it together as a community.

03 **Build regular touchpoints into your weekly routine:** Repurpose things you already do to serve a double function. Go to the gym with another community member. Schedule a standing Saturday morning group run or playdate at the park. Sit together at church. Join the same book club. Take an online course together.

04 **Host Sabbath dinners:** Start inviting over a few close friends or family you can really relax with for a Sabbath feast. Make it celebratory. Practice gratitude, share highlights of the week, sing a song, sit around a firepit, and rejoice together in God.

05   **Begin therapy:** Find a trusted Christian counselor and begin the journey of healing from your past in order to more deeply enter into relationships of mutual trust and love.

06   **Go through more Practices together:** Visit practicingtheway.org to consider running the Practicing the Way course or another one of our nine Practices.

07   **Move closer to each other:** Consider moving to be closer to brothers and sisters you sense God is spiritually adopting you to. Community is all about proximity. The closer you are, the easier and more spontaneous life together can actually be. The farther apart, the more difficult. If appropriate, consider becoming roommates, moving into the same apartment complex or onto the same street, living in multigenerational housing, or adopting more radical ideas like co-housing or homesteading.

# Recommended Reading

Here are some of our favorite books on the Practice of community for those of you who desire to learn more:

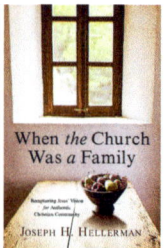

### *When the Church Was a Family* by Joseph Hellerman

An incredible book on the biblical and cultural meaning of *family* in the New Testament. It paints a compelling picture of the church as a "strong group" community in a culture of radical individualism.

### *The Life We're Looking For* by Andy Crouch

A beautiful vision of life in community in the digital age, with an inspiring chapter on kinship groups.

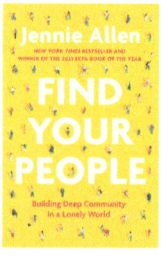

### *Find Your People* by Jennie Allen

An honest look at how to find and form community in our transient time that is both inspirational and pragmatic.

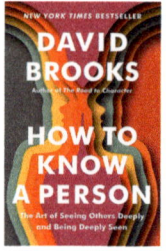

### *How to Know a Person* by David Brooks

An exploration of really learning to listen and love another soul.

**The Band Meeting by Kevin Watson and Scott Kisker**

A short, compelling summary of both the Methodist discipleship band model and the heart of true Christian community.

*Made to Belong* **by David Kim**

Our recommended reading for this Practice and an excellent overview of finding belonging in community.

*The Relational Soul* **by Richard Plass and James Cofield**

A stunning introduction to attachment theory and spiritual formation.

*The Other Half of Church* **by Jim Wilder and Michel Hendricks**

A provocative take on the need for a whole-brain, relational approach to discipleship, based on easy-to-read overviews of recent learnings from neuroscience.

*Relational Spirituality* **by Todd Hall with M. Elizabeth Lewis Hall**

An in-depth, academic work that is best read with a few others, this is a seminal book on the relational nature of spiritual formation.

# The Practices

Information alone isn't enough to produce transformation.

By adopting not just the teaching but also the practices from Jesus' own life, we open up our entire beings to God and allow him to transform us into people of love.

Our nine core Practices work together to form a Rule of Life for the modern era.

| | | |
|---|---|---|
| **Sabbath** | **Prayer** | **Fasting** |
| **Solitude** | **Generosity** | **Scripture** |
| **Community** | **Service** | **Witness** |

### WHAT'S INCLUDED FOR EACH PRACTICE

**Four Sessions**

Each session includes teaching, guided discussion, and weekly exercises to integrate the Practices into daily life.

**Companion Guide**

A detailed guide provides question prompts, session-by-session exercises, and space to write and reflect.

**Recommended Resources**

Additional recommended readings and podcasts to get the most out of the Practices.

Learn more by visiting practicingtheway.org/resources.

The Community Practice

# The Practicing the Way Course

An eight-session primer on spiritual formation.

Two thousand years ago, Jesus said to his disciples, "Follow me." But what does it mean for us to follow Jesus today?

The Practicing the Way Course is an on-ramp to spiritual formation, exploring what it means to follow Jesus and laying the foundation for a life of apprenticeship to him.

## WHAT'S INCLUDED

### Eight Sessions

John Mark and other voices teaching on apprenticing under Jesus, spiritual formation, healing from sin, meeting God in pain, crafting a Rule of Life, living in community, and more

### Exercises

Weekly practices and exercises to help integrate what you've learned into your everyday life

### Guided Conversations

Prompts to reflect on your experience and process honestly in community

### Companion Guide

A detailed workbook with exercises, space to write and reflect, and suggestions for supplemental resources

Learn more by visiting practicingtheway.org/resources.

# Practicing the Way:
*Be with him. Become like him. Do as he did.*

The first followers of Jesus developed a Rule of Life, or habits and practices based on the life of Jesus himself. As they learned to live like their teacher, they became people who made space for God to do his most transformative work in their lives.

*Practicing the Way* is a vision for the future, shaped by the wisdom of the past. It's an introduction to spiritual formation accessible to both beginners and lifelong followers of Jesus, and a companion to the Practicing the Way Course. This book offers theological substance, astute cultural insight, and practical wisdom for creating a Rule of Life in the modern age.

You can order your copy or get copies for your community at practicingtheway.org/book or through your preferred bookseller.

The Community Practice

# The Circle

Practicing the Way is a nonprofit that develops spiritual formation resources for churches and small groups learning how to become apprentices in the Way of Jesus.

We believe one of the greatest needs of our time is for people to discover how to become lifelong disciples of Jesus. To that end, we help people learn how to be with Jesus, become like him, and do as he did, through the practices and rhythms he and his earliest followers lived by.

All of our downloadable ministry resources are available at no cost, thanks to the generosity of The Circle and other givers from around the world who partner with us to see formation integrated into the church at large.

To learn more or join us, visit practicingtheway.org/give.

# For Facilitators

Before you begin, there are three easy things you need to do. (This should only take 10–15 minutes.)

01   Go to launch.practicingtheway.org, log in, create a group, and send a digital invitation to your community. This will give your group access to the Spiritual Health Reflection, videos, and all sorts of valuable extras. Encourage your group to bring along their Companion Guides to each session, as these contain the discussion questions and space to take notes.

   ○ You can purchase a print or ebook version from your preferred retailer or find a free digital PDF version at launch.practicingtheway.org. We recommend the print version so you can stay away from your devices during the Practices, as well as take notes during each session. But we realize that digital works better for some.

   ○ Note: You can order the Guides ahead of time and have them waiting when people arrive for Session 01, or encourage people to order or download their own and bring them to your gatherings.

02   Send a message to your group encouraging everyone to take the Spiritual Health Reflection before your first gathering, which can be found at launch.practicingtheway.org.

03   If your group has not been through the Practicing the Way Course, invite them to watch the short primer in the online Dashboard before you gather for Session 01 of this Practice.

For training, tips, and more resources for facilitating the Community Practice, log in to the Dashboard at launch.practicingtheway.org.

APPENDIX

# Bonus Conversations

For those of you who want to spend longer sitting in this Practice, we've included an additional four weeks of material in this Guide to go deeper in Scripture and discussion.

You are welcome to pause in between sessions for these additional conversations, or to skip over them.

Explore some of the additional resources available for the Community Practice on our platform at launch.practicingtheway.org.

# Be Family Around a Table

We all feel the divisiveness of our present moment. It seems increasingly true that the more different we are—be it politically, socioeconomically, religiously, or racially—the less likely we are to be in relationship with one another, let alone be in the same room. These days, differences and divisions often blur together. Sadly, the same can be true in the church, where we can be tempted to prioritize other allegiances over our shared kinship as siblings in God's family.

In the time Paul lived, this kind of divisiveness was as true religiously as it was culturally. That's why Paul is so clear in his letter to the Ephesian church: Jesus has created one new family. The question is: Despite our differences, will we live like that is true?

## Read Ephesians 2v11–22

## Discuss the Scripture

01    What most stands out to you from this text?

02    Reflect on what this text has to say about your previous position before
      being adopted into God's family. What thoughts or feelings emerge for you?

03    What differences seem to create division in our surrounding culture? What
      about in church community? How are they similar or different?

04    What barriers do you experience to seeing someone as your brother or
      sister in Christ? What invitation do you sense there from this text?

## Discuss the practice

01    Describe what sharing a meal looked like for you this week.

02    What was one of the feelings you experienced going into the meal, and did
      that feeling change throughout or after your time together? If so, how?

03    What about the time sharing a meal felt ordinary? Why do you think it is
      important to embrace the ordinary nature of these meals?

04    What resistance do you experience, if any, to the idea of sharing a weekly
      meal in community? What is compelling about it?

## Repeat the exercise

This week's exercise is to share a meal together. If you are here, it likely means
that your group has decided to gather together for these Bonus Conversations
in addition to the four sessions. We encourage you to begin these gatherings
together just as you would a regular session for this Practice—around a table
with a good meal.

# Share Your Joys and Sorrows

After spending the better part of his letter to the Roman Church recounting Jesus' mercy and grace, Paul makes a turn in chapter 12 to how we are to respond to such good news. For Paul, our response is certainly not a solo effort; rather, he writes a list of exhortations that can be seen almost like "house rules" for the family of God. In today's Scripture, for every encouragement in this list that can be lived out individually, there are almost two commands that require other people. Paul makes it clear that our response to God's mercy unfolds in the context of relationships—one meal, one open door, one shared tear at a time.

## Read Romans 12v9–16

## Discuss the Scripture

01    Which verse in the text most stands out to you, and why?

02    Share about a time when you were on the receiving end of a person living out one of these verses. How did that impact you?

03    What part of this text seems most countercultural or radical in our present moment, and why?

04    Consider one piece of this text you can put into practice this week. Which part is it, and what are you wanting to do?

## Discuss the practice

01    Describe how sharing your highs and lows around the table went at your last meal.

02    What feelings did you experience as different people shared? Joy? Compassion? Sadness?

03    What felt natural or unnatural about this exercise?

04    What themes or patterns did you notice as you went around the table, if any? How has this exercise impacted your view on the importance of honesty in community?

## Repeat the exercise

We encourage you to share highs and lows during your meal together as a way to continue growing in trust and connection with one another. You might even consider following up with someone later in the week about what they shared if that would be suitable and helpful. Remember, transformation begins not from where we think we *should* be, but from where we *actually* are. Sharing a personal celebration and challenge you're facing is a great starting place for bringing more of your honest self to your community.

# Confess Your Sins

As humans, there's perhaps nothing we desire more than to be fully loved. But to experience that depth of love, we have to bring our whole selves—"warts and all"—before someone we trust. To truly be loved, we must first take the risk of being fully known.

In today's Scripture, we see two paths described: walking in the light and walking in the darkness. For John, the light, though exposing, is where God's love and forgiveness can actually get into us. The dark, however, is where we don't just believe, but live, lies. It's in the shadows of our lives that sin and shame find oxygen. As the saying goes, "We are only as sick as our secrets."

So how do we change paths? John puts one simple and courageous action at the threshold separating darkness and light: The invitation, in his words, is to "confess our sins."

## Read 1 John 1v5–10

## Discuss the Scripture

01   What stands out to you about the difference in what this text says about walking in the light compared to the darkness?

02   In what ways does thinking about "fellowship" in the context of confession deepen your view of what that word means?

03   How does this text match up with your personal experience of confession? How is it different?

04   How might the realities stated in this text about what is available in the light influence how you receive someone's confession?

## Discuss the practice

01   Whom did you decide to confess your sin to, and what qualities does that person possess that made you choose them?

02   How would you describe what your experience of being vulnerable in community has been like in the past?

03   What fears, hopes, or expectations did you have going into this exercise?

04   What was the difference between how you felt going into and how you felt coming out of your time of confession?

## Repeat the exercise

This week's exercise is to reconnect with your confessor and confess your sins from the week. While confession is not an easy practice and requires no small amount of courage, our goal as apprentices to Jesus should be to grow toward bringing our sin into the light more frequently. Some people go so far as to have quick check-ins over the phone each morning. While that might seem far off from what you can see yourself doing now, start by confessing again this week, and consider how you might make this a more regular practice in your life.

# Stay Together to Grow

In more than half of Paul's letters to first-century churches, he encourages the communities to exercise patience, and nearly a third address their need to forgive one another. We can often view the Early Church through the rose-colored glasses of Acts chapter 2 and overlook the relational strife these communities were constantly navigating.

There is no such thing as life in the family of God that doesn't require patience, forgiveness, and all the attributes we read in today's Scripture. For Paul, the real question was this: Are we willing to keep "putting on" the attributes that will transform us into people of love?

## Read Colossians 3v12–14

## Discuss the Scripture

01   Which of the attributes from verse 12 do you feel most compelled to live into currently?

02   How have you been personally impacted by someone extending forgiveness toward you?

03   What are a few ways you can practically "put on love" in your community on a regular basis?

04   How might living this text enable you to stay rooted and committed to your community?

## Discuss the practice

01   Share one of your responses from the guided reflection in Session 04.

02   Which session or exercise from this Practice was the most impactful for you personally, and why?

03   Reflecting on the past few weeks in this Practice, in what ways have you seen your relationship to community change?

04   If you could share only one insight or reflection that you want to internalize going forward from this Practice, what would it be?

## Repeat the exercise

For our final week we are working on our plan for next steps to living in community. We invite you to revisit the reflection questions on page 86 this week and continue to prayerfully listen for God's direction. Focus especially on translating what you hear into action. We hope that as you reflect on your time in the Community Practice, you begin to see that although living in community is not easy, when pursued with intentionality and commitment, it has the potential to deeply change your life for the better.

*01 14*

To inquire about ordering this Companion Guide in
bulk quantities for your church, small group, or staff,
contact churches@penguinrandomhouse.com.